The Cult I Left
Amy Jacobson, as told to
Julia Anshasi

Giant Publishing Company
Lincoln, Nebraska, USA

2025 by Julia Anshasi

Published by Giant Publishing Company
Post Office Box 6455
Lincoln, NE 68506
www.giantpublishingcompany.com

Printed in the United States of America

All rights reserved. No part of this publication may be used or reproduced in any form or by any electronic or mechanical means, including information storage and retrieval systems, without permission in writing from the publisher.

All scripture quotations are from the King James Version of the Bible, unless otherwise noted.

Library of Congress Cataloging-in-Publication Data
Anshasi, Julia, 1963 -
The Cult I Left   Self-help/Julia Anshasi
   1. Christianity
   2. Self-help

ISBN 979-8-9898098-1-3
TX0009479510

Books by Julia Anshasi

Broken ~ Poems from the Holy Spirit
Copyright 2017 – Winner of the 2021 Illumination Book Awards Silver Medal

Some Things are HOT! Some Things are NOT!
Copyright 2018

Behind the Word: Bible Stories to Ignite Your Imagination
Copyright 2018

Why Did the Dinosaurs Die?
Copyright 2019

Winter in Eden
Copyright 2020 – Winner of the 2022 Illumination Book Awards Bronze Medal

The Revelation of Jesus Christ
Copyright 2020

Books by Julia Anshasi, continued

One Part Nonsense
Copyright 2020

Forgiving Yourself
Copyright 2021

Spiritual Exhaustion
Copyright 2021 – Winner of the 2022 Illumination Book Awards Silver Medal

Lame for Life
Copyright 2022

Quiet ~ A devotional
Copyright 2023

Unbearable Loneliness
Copyright 2024

7 Things God Hates
Copyright 2024

Table of Contents

Introduction

Chapter 1: The love………………………….Page 7

Chapter 2: The work……..………............Page 21

Chapter 3: The money…………………......Page 31

Chapter 4: The lies…………………..……….Page 49

Chapter 5: The awakening………………......Page 61

Chapter 6: The revelations………………...Page 77

After word

Introduction

I met Amy Jacobson in January of 2024. Amy had sought me out because she knew I was a local book publisher, and she had read some of my work.

At our first meeting, she dropped her bombshell question: "What do you know about cults?" I was taken aback, and had to answer truthfully. "Not much," I replied.

Amy took some time to take stock of me – trying to decide if she should trust me with her story, or not. She is a very quiet person, but eventually began opening up to me. I was riveted by what she had experienced. Shocked, horrified, fascinated, repulsed, saddened, angered – it is truly difficult to describe the emotions that overwhelmed me as I heard her recount the eleven years she had spent in a cult.

I told Amy that her story needed to be made public. She seemed fearful at times, almost as though she was looking over her shoulder, both figuratively and literally. At one point she hung her head and said, barely above a whisper, "What if something happens to me?" I asked her what might happen to others if she didn't tell her story. I believe it was that question that gave Amy the courage to finally speak out.

This is Amy's true story. For this book, she asked me to change certain details regarding the group she joined, including names, locations, and identifying characteristics, in order to protect the safety and privacy of those involved. ~ Julia Anshasi

Chapter 1: The love

It was a hot summer's day, and I was in a bad mood. Everything seemed to be going wrong. I had been cleaning my house, and I wasn't in the mood for that, either.

God, I need something new to happen in my life! Every day is the same old, same old. What is Your plan? What do You want me to do?

My whiny prayer was answered by a knock at the door. I opened it to find a stranger on my doorstep with a flyer in his hand.

"Good morning!" he greeted me cheerfully. "I am in your neighborhood today, inviting you to attend a service at my church."

My ears perked up. I had been less than thrilled with the church I had been attending. Maybe this was the answer to my prayer.

"What kind of church is it?" I asked, glancing at the flyer. On the cover was a glossy photograph of a good-looking couple, with their bios.

"Oh, our pastors are great!" he replied enthusiastically. "They're originally from Guatemala, and they felt the Lord calling them to the United States to minister to the people here. They are so humble, and so deep into the Word."

That sounded fantastic to me. The various churches I had attended since moving to this city seemed very short on the Word. I was intrigued.

After the man left, I read through the flyer several times. *Maybe I should give it a try,* I thought. If it doesn't work out, or if it's not for me, I can always just not go back.

The following Sunday I stood in front of my closet, fussing about what to wear. Since this was a new church for me, I felt I should make an effort to look nice. I had never agreed with the modern evangelical trend of wearing your shabbiest clothing to church. But I also didn't want to draw a lot of attention to myself. I finally settled on a plain black skirt that went down to my ankles, and a plain white shirt. *This should help me to blend in,* I thought.

As I pulled into the parking lot, I observed people getting out of their vehicles and walking into the building. The church was currently meeting in the basement of a retail store. Everyone was dressed very nicely. I began to have a bit of a qualm, but quickly squelched it and made my way inside.

On the threshold of the main room, my small qualm mushroomed into a huge anxiety cloud. The women were all dressed in floor-length, sparkly gowns. I glanced down at my plain black-and-white ensemble and headed for the back row.

"Amy!" I turned to see the man who had given me the flyer on my doorstep. "So glad you could make it! Let me make you some hot chocolate." He disappeared into the kitchen.

I took stock of my surroundings. In the front row, four elderly white women were sitting and chatting with one another. In every other seat, a Mexican person smiled back at me.

I felt a sinking feeling in my stomach. *What if they don't accept me?* I thought. It had never occurred to me that the pastors on the front of the glossy flyer would be ministering only to Mexicans. In my naïveté, I had thought (or actually not even given it a thought) that the church would be comprised of people of all races, like the other churches I had attended.

Taking a deep breath, I looked around again. True, the four elderly women in the front row were white. Obviously, the congregation had accepted them. Clearly, I was making an issue out of nothing.

As a white person, I had experienced racial discrimination only once that I could remember. It had left me with a very uneasy feeling, but it had also been an "aha!" moment which made me more determined than ever to never judge another human being by outward appearance.

Years earlier, I had walked into a fast-food barbeque place, looking to get some take-out food. The handsome Mexican man behind the counter made eye contact with me as I stepped up to read the menu. There were two cute Mexican teenage girls standing nearby, giggling and smiling at him.

After studying the menu, I made eye contact with the man again. Other than the two girls, there was no one else in the restaurant. He glanced at me and quickly looked away. *Huh?* I thought. I took a half step forward. The girls, who had already placed their orders, were still giggling and flirting with him. He made eye contact with me a third time. I nervously cleared my throat and said, "I would like – "

One of the girls immediately began talking loudly, drowning out my voice. He glanced at her, then back to me, then at her again. The girls giggled and elbowed each other.

It suddenly dawned on me that I was not welcome in this restaurant. The man behind the counter was not going to take my order.

A flood of embarrassment swept over me, and I quickly turned and almost ran out of the door. Sitting in my car in the parking lot, I decided to go with Chinese food instead.

Somehow, I had broken an unwritten rule. This was a restaurant that was staffed by and frequented by Mexicans. White people were not allowed.

Lest anyone think I felt victimized over this, let me assure you, I didn't. It was just a wake-up call to me that in spite of the tremendous strides made in racial relations in the United States, some people hadn't yet read the memo.

But nothing even remotely like that was happening at this church! One by one, the congregation came up to me and introduced themselves. Everyone was smiling and welcoming as they shook my hand. My unfounded fears melted away.

As I listened to the sermon, I felt the power of God fill the room. This preacher was no-nonsense. He didn't beat around the bush or sugarcoat anything.

Afterwards, it was announced that a church meal had been planned for after the service. I felt a bit awkward, since I had brought nothing, but my new friends assured me that there was plenty of food to go around, and there was. I was amazed at the authentic Guatemalan and Mexican dishes that were served – so delicious and such a welcome change from the bland American food I usually ate. Several of the older Mexican ladies smiled shyly at me, and sneaked more spoonsful of food onto my plate. There was definitely a language barrier, but I smiled at them, and they smiled at me, and I discovered that a smile is the same in every language.

The pastors came and sat down near me, and welcomed me to the church. I asked a lot of questions, and they seemed very open and willing to share with me. I learned that Pastor Richard had had a very successful ministry in Guatemala, until the day the Lord told him to go to the United States. "I didn't want to go," he said frankly. "I argued with the Lord for several days about it, and then I finally surrendered."

Pastor Leah, his wife, listened intently as he spoke. "I didn't want to go, either," she said. "But the Lord confirmed it so many times, we knew we would have to obey."

I took in what they were saying, while at the same time being aware of snippets of other conversations all around me in Spanish, and various South America dialects. The younger people in the church, as is usually the case, spoke perfect English, but many of the older people did not.

One thing that immediately struck me about this church was the overwhelming love and sense of camaraderie that I felt. One of the young women offered to give a ride to one of the elderly ladies. Someone else dished up a plate of food and wrapped it up for another elderly woman to take home.

Everyone was kind and thoughtful, and love seemed to ooze out of every corner of the room.

As things were winding down, I decided that I would make myself useful by washing dishes and clearing plates. I marveled at the elegant dresses the women were wearing, and laughed at myself as I realized that of all the outfits there, mine was the most suitable for washing dishes.

I left that day with an overwhelming feeling of love and security, basking in the glow of new friendships and the possibility of a bright future as a new member of Boundless Horizons Church. I just had one pressing problem: Where could I get some inexpensive sparkly dresses?

***

Almost immediately, I met Guadalupe, a young woman in the church. She and I hit it off right away. She was beautiful, funny, smart, and deeply in love with Jesus Christ. She and I spent many hours together, dreaming, planning, praying, and talking - about everything and nothing.

Guadalupe was one of the many people in the church who demonstrated to me that prayer is not something that is done once in a while, or when a person is in a desperate situation. Rather, it is a constant, daily way of life. She prayed every time she left my presence, asking God for His protection and blessings over me. I had never experienced that before.

Pastors Richard and Leah showered me with love and acceptance. Having grown up in an extremely dysfunctional home, and attending an equally dysfunctional church in my home town, walking through the doors of this church for me was like Dorothy walking out of her black-and-white Kansas world, into the colorful and glittering Land of Oz.

The pastors impressed upon all of us that indeed, anything was possible to him who believed (Mark 9:23). The contrast between Boundless Horizons and the church I grew up in was stark. I had always been taught that when you pray, you pray for God's will to be done. At my new church, we were told to ask God for anything, anything at all, and if we believed, He would give us what we asked for. 'Crazy faith' is what they called it.

I felt joined to the pastors and the other church members with ties of love that I didn't even know could exist.

I drew them with cords of a man, with bands of love: and I was to them as they that take off the yoke on their jaws, and I laid meat unto them. Hosea 11:4

The people in this church took serving others very seriously. I was, and still am to this day, amazed at the care that everyone showed for each other.

One Friday, I had invited a family member over to my house to celebrate his birthday with a special meal. But as the day wore on, I began to feel very sick. I left work early and lay down on my couch, thinking I could recover enough to get up and start cooking. But I just felt worse and worse. In desperation, I called Hannah, one of the young women in the church. I explained the situation to her.

"Can you come over and cook? Everything is already chopped up and prepared; it just needs to be cooked."

Hannah said she would be right over. And true to her word, she was. She cooked everything, plated it up, brought me a cold drink, and left right before my guest arrived. I had tears in my eyes as I thanked her. She brushed off my thanks with a smile.

"You would do the same for me," she said.

I absolutely marveled at her kindness to me. Would I do the same for her (or anyone)? I would like to think so. But in reality, I might refuse, because I wouldn't want to expose myself to her germs!

I lay on the couch while the birthday boy ate his delicious meal. Although it was not the evening I had planned, it had been rescued by my dear Hannah.

It would be impossible to list all the acts of love that I experienced and witnessed at Boundless Horizons, but here are a few:

- The church paid for a replacement used car for one of the elderly women whose car was beyond repair.
- Pastor Leah opened her own wallet and gave money to a church member, when she herself was very short on cash, so the church member could start her own business.
- Both pastors met with me several times, at their suggestion, to lay hands on me and pray for me when I was feeling especially down.
- Both pastors frequently went without food and sleep during times of intense spiritual warfare, praying for the church.

But not everyone was feeling the love. After I had been with the church for about a year, there was a dramatic walk-out by one of the members, complete with slanderous gossip and a lot of ugly words. This man left and took almost all of the furniture and sound equipment with him. I was shocked.

I heard through the grapevine that Pastor Richard had called the police, and he, the man who left, and the police had gathered in the parking lot for a very loud conversation. This confused me.

"Did you really call the cops?" I asked Pastor Richard the next time I saw him. He nodded.

"Yes, this needed to be handled by the police," he said.

"But the Bible says that if you have a problem with someone in the church, you're not supposed to get the law involved (1 Corinthians 6: 5 – 7)," I argued.

I could see that Pastor Richard was annoyed by what I'd said. In the years to come, I would observe that he did not take kindly to anyone having a different interpretation of scripture than his own.

"Carlos needs to know that what he did was wrong," he said shortly. I didn't have the confidence to say any more.

Shortly after this, Guadalupe stopped by my house for dinner one night. She was very subdued – not at all her usual cheerful self. We sat in silence after our meal. Finally, she spoke.

"No one is happy," she said, a single tear rolling down her cheek. "Things aren't like they used to be. We used to linger and talk after services; now people just rush out the door. The atmosphere has changed."

"Yes, it has," I agreed. "I still can't believe that Carlos said all those things about the pastors and the church! How long had he been feeling that way? Why didn't he sit down and talk with them? I don't understand people sometimes!" The more I talked, the more agitated I became.

Guadalupe sighed. "Pastor Richard is a man of faith," she said sadly. "But he is also very stubborn. Sometimes, when people think about faith, they can't tell the difference between faith and fantasy."

I was to remember her words later.

At the next service, Pastor Richard had a warning for the congregation. "Touch not mine anointed, and do my prophets no harm (1 Chronicles 16: 22)." He scanned every face in front of him with a piercing gaze.

"When certain people leave this church, they feel like they can spread lies about us, and get others to turn against us," he said firmly, looking at each person in turn. "But God will deal with the people who do this. They will not prosper. They will not succeed. Some of them will lose their lives."

I squirmed in my seat. Lose their lives? That seemed a little extreme. I raised my hand.

"Pastor, did you talk with Carlos? Did you ask him what was going on? We all love Carlos – it hurts that he left so suddenly under such bad terms. I think if the two of you would sit down and talk, I know you could come to some kind of peace between you."

I was nervous and embarrassed about saying this out loud, but I know others were thinking the same thing.

Now Pastor Richard's gaze was fixed on me alone. "We don't sit down and have a meeting with the devil," he said, his eyes blazing. "I have turned him over to God for discipline, and God will avenge me."

This was a turning point in the church, one of many to come. It was almost as if the pastors were saying, "Are you for us, or against us?" Those who questioned the way Carlos left, and the resultant fallout from his departure, fell into the camp of "against" the pastors. And those who didn't question it and chose to never mention it, fell into the camp of "for" the pastors.

After Pastor Richard's scathing denunciation, the love at the church ramped up, if anything. Both pastors called me in to pray with me, both listened while I told of various problems I was having in my life, and both displayed so much love to me that at times it seemed almost super-human.

It hurt that Carlos had left the way he did. But I soon forgot about him. Clearly, he was not committed to the ministry as the rest of us were. If God was going to punish him, I just needed to stand aside.

I felt grateful that my pastors loved me, and grateful to be a part of a community, even if other, ungrateful people didn't feel the same way, and left the church.

Why do these people love me so much? I asked myself this question many, many times. I never got a clear answer, but the unfailing love they showed to me made me all the more determined to love them, and serve them, in any way I could.

Chapter 2: The work

Pastor Richard called a meeting of the church one Sunday afternoon. I felt a bit of trepidation, wondering what it was about.

"Pastor Leah and I have been praying," he began. "We need to re-assign some duties and titles."

We all listened politely, knowing that he was referring to Carlos' angry departure from the church. I wondered why I had been called to this meeting. It really had nothing to do with me.

He went on. "Hope, you are the new director of evangelism. Katherine, you are the new church secretary. Della, you are the new worship director. And Amy, you are the new church treasurer."

My mouth fell open. Church treasurer? Oh, no. I was not qualified to do that. I stared at him in dismay.

He read my thoughts. "Don't ever say, 'I'm not qualified to do this or that,' he said firmly. "God will qualify you for whatever He has called you to do."

I swallowed hard. I knew that my pastors saw things in the spiritual realm that other people didn't see. If God had told them that I was to be the church treasurer, who was I to argue with God?

But I felt extreme apprehension about the new role that had been thrust upon me.

As I lay in bed that night, I thought about it again and again. I felt a certain amount of resentment at being told that I was the treasurer – not asked. And I felt a ton of guilt at feeling resentful. I didn't want to let the pastors down, after all they had done for me.

God, if this is truly what You want me to do, please give me the grace and the ability to do it!

Eventually I drifted off to sleep.

As church treasurer, I discovered a lot of things that I wished I did not have to discover. An elderly woman had held the position before me, and if I thought I was unqualified, she most certainly was. I discovered cash shoved into drawers in the church office, cash that had never been removed from offering envelopes, bank deposit amounts that didn't match up with what was recorded, and many other messes. I had my work cut out for me. I also was beginning to see why Pastor Richard had retired her from her duties, and assigned them to me.

I truly don't believe there was any dishonesty involved; I just think the job was too much for her.

It was too much for me, too, but I kept at it. Within a few months, the books were in order, everything was recorded properly, and I was beginning to breathe a bit more easily. I was worried, though, about the way the finances were handled. I shared my concerns with Pastor Leah.

"It's not a good idea to have one person gather the offering, count the offering, record the offering, and take it to the bank," I attempted to explain to her. "These duties should be split up among two or three people – it's just good accounting practice."

Pastor Leah looked at me as though I had two heads. "Pastor Richard has complete trust in you," she said quietly. "He has never said he wants anyone else involved."

"But what if I make a mistake?" I argued. "I'm only human. What if I miscount something, or misplace the deposit?"

"You will not make a mistake," she smiled encouragingly. "We trust you."

Although I certainly appreciated my pastors' unwavering trust, the burden of making sure everything was correct, all the time, weighed heavily on my shoulders. But I squared those shoulders up. I was determined to make them proud of me.

***

Pastor Leah was about to deliver her second child, and I asked if I could take over cleaning the church building, something she had always done. She gratefully accepted my offer. This was something I knew I could do, without a problem, and it didn't involve much thought or precision, as being treasurer did.

Being the cleaning lady also revealed certain things to me that I had not been aware of before. The supplies that every church needs – communion wine and wafers, cleaning supplies, paper towels for the restrooms, tissues and toilet paper, were pretty much non-existent. As I stood in the kitchen one day, surveying the empty cupboards, I realized that someone needed to go to the grocery store. And that someone would have to be me. I began supplying the needed items from my own pocket.

Pastor Leah was very much aware of the church's financial deficit. She started two businesses within a year of each other, and recruited the young women in the church to work for her. She also asked me to do the bookkeeping for her businesses.

Not again! I screamed silently. "Yes, of course," I said out loud.

We all began putting in many, many hours, working for Pastor Leah.

To this day, I still don't understand why it is so hard for anyone to tell Pastor Leah no. She is determined, yes. Full of faith, yes. Kind and loving, certainly. It is something that I just can't put my finger on, but it is almost impossible to say no to her.

At first, business number one brought in quite a bit of money. All of her workers got paid, except me. I kept doing her bookkeeping for free.

Business number two brought in a small amount of money, which got progressively smaller as time went on. None of the workers got paid, and this was a huge problem.

I wondered if Pastor Leah was familiar with Department of Labor regulations. I guessed that she wasn't. I felt it was my duty to warn her.

"If someone files a complaint with the DOL, your business could be fined thousands of dollars for not paying your workers," I said cautiously. She stared at me in shock.

"They will get paid," she said firmly. "My business is about to explode, and everyone will get paid what is due to them."

I said nothing further. Clearly God had spoken to her, and once again, who was I to contradict God?

Besides working for her two businesses, we were all very busy working for the church. Setting up media equipment, taking it down, cleaning, preparing food, setting up chairs in the sanctuary, doing children's ministry, looking after the pastors' children…I sometimes felt that church was a never-ending merry-go-round of work. I always rebuked myself for having these thoughts.

How do you think the pastors feel? I argued with myself. *They stay up all night praying for you, fool, and then come to church and give you the Word. You should be grateful.*

And I was grateful. As the burdens of work and church increased, I reminded myself of all I had to be grateful for. These people would not hesitate to take a bullet for me. I knew that. And I would not hesitate to take a bullet for them. What we all had at Boundless Horizons was unique. We had the kind of fellowship that the early church had had – something that is so rare as to be almost non-existent today.

And all that believed were together, and had all things common; And sold their possessions and goods, and parted them to all men, as every man had need. Acts 2: 44 – 45

And the needs were great.

The young women in the church spent a lot of time at the pastors' house, cleaning, preparing food, and looking after their children. Pastor Leah, while being the strongest person spiritually that I had ever met, was physically very fragile. She was frequently hospitalized, and the church always stepped in to help her family. I began to see that doing bookkeeping for free was nothing compared to providing free child care! I was thankful that they had never asked me to do that. I think they instinctively knew that their children would not survive intact even one hour with me.

Some people are good with children. Others are not.

In addition to being the church treasurer and cleaning lady, I was in charge of security, taught the new believers' class, helped with baptisms, set up and took down communion, set up cameras, sang on the worship team, did the public Bible readings, printed offering envelopes, and was guest preacher when the pastors asked me to preach. My duties increased until I felt I was going to collapse.

I looked around at the other church members, wondering if they felt the same way. They had even more on their plates than I did. But no one ever said anything, at least not to me. I suspected that they wouldn't, anyway. As much as they loved me, and I know they truly did, I was not a part of their culture. Any complaints they had would most likely be discussed among themselves.

Every group has its unwritten rules, and Boundless Horizons was no different. One unwritten rule was the length of the song service. We would usually sing for an hour or an hour and a half. I love singing to

Jesus, but that seemed a bit too much to me, because of the heels. Heels were required!

Standing up front, singing into the microphone, wearing my three-inch heels, I would always long for the song service to be over. As I said, I love singing, and I've been known to walk around my house (in my slippers) belting out worship songs to Him. But man, those heels were killing me. The young women wore even higher heels than I did.

But I must confess that I rebelled a few times and wore flats. I also noticed several people kicking off their shoes and going barefooted half-way through the service. Something about that always made me smile.

The other issue with the music was the volume. It was always at an ear-splitting level. I wore earplugs most of the time when I was in church. I seemed to be the only person who was bothered with the volume level, so I just inserted my ear plugs and kept my mouth shut.

One time a new couple visited our church, and I greeted them at the door. Pastor Richard came out of his office and started talking with the three of us. The man politely asked if the music could be turned down, because he was having a problem hearing what we were saying. I was secretly glad that he asked that. But Pastor Richard said, "Oh, you think it's too loud?" and went on with the conversation, making no move to turn the music down.

I learned later that Pastor Leah preferred the music at a very high volume, because it helped her to tune in to what the Holy Spirit was saying.

Regarding what the Holy Spirit was saying, we were often engaged in work that was actively undoing work that we had done before. For example, after hanging beautiful pictures on the walls of the sanctuary, at the pastors' request, I was surprised to see the pictures gone shortly thereafter. I learned that Pastor Leah had been told by the Holy Spirit that it was time to get rid of the pictures (although they had been there less than a month) and get new ones. This upset me, because it had been a lot of work to hang them, but I reasoned that if the Holy Spirit had said to get rid of them, we needed to get rid of them.

***

I began shutting my phone off when I went to bed at night. Pastor Richard and Leah would text at all hours, and I just didn't want to deal with it. I felt I was being very selfish, but didn't see a way to change that part of my personality. They get by on very little sleep, and they have always operated that way, but I need my eight hours if I am to function at all the next day.

One of the young women asked me one time why I didn't attend the overnight prayer meetings. I explained my need for sleep.

Am I the only person in this church who sleeps? I began to wonder. *Everyone else seems to be working and on call twenty-four hours a day.*

The huge workload and lack of sleep did take its toll, however. More than once I saw someone sleeping through the Sunday morning service. I'm sure the pastors saw it too, but they did not publicly embarrass anyone, thankfully.

I remained very uncomfortable about the unpaid wages from Pastor Leah's business, but I put it in the Lord's hands. There was nothing I could do about that.

"The Lord will not allow anyone to speak against His anointed." I'd heard my pastors say this on multiple occasions. They always warned that sickness, bankruptcy, and death would come to those who criticized the ministry.

So I didn't.

Chapter 3: The money

One of the things that was often taught at Boundless Horizons was that church members should own their own businesses. "If you work for someone else," Pastor Richard often said, "You are a slave to that person. If you own your own business, you are the master! You are the boss! You can come and go as you please, and leave the work to other people. That frees you up to do the work of the ministry."

Having never heard this concept before, I was intrigued. I was also skeptical. The people that I had known who were self-employed put in much more than forty hours a week. Most were on call twenty-four seven. After all, if you are the boss, you are responsible for everything. I wondered what kind of business would allow the boss to be free, while others did the work.

"I am raising up millionaires!" Pastor Richard exhorted all of us. "Each one of you has a business idea inside of you. Come to me, and I will pray over you and over your idea, and release God's blessings on your business."

I tried very hard to believe this. Wouldn't it be great to be a millionaire? Think about what you could do with that money.

"Some people accuse me of preaching the prosperity gospel," he said. "That's all right. You remain over there, and preach the poverty gospel. Me, I will stay over here and preach the prosperity gospel."

That always made me smile.

The Bible has a lot to say about money.

Two things have I required of thee; deny me them not before I die: Remove far from me vanity and lies: give me neither poverty nor riches; feed me with food convenient for me: Lest I be full, and deny thee, and say, Who is the Lord? or lest I be poor, and steal, and take the name of my God in vain. Proverbs 30: 7-9

This was always how I had thought about money. I wanted "just enough." I didn't want to be rich, and I didn't want to be poor.

And having food and raiment let us be therewith content. 1 Timothy 6: 8

My pastors thought about money very differently.

Beloved, I wish above all things that thou mayest prosper and be in health, even as thy soul prospereth. 3 John 1: 3

"God wants us to prosper! He wants us to be rich!" Pastor Richard declared.

For ye know the grace of our Lord Jesus Christ, that, though he was rich, yet for your sakes he became poor, that ye through his poverty might be rich. 2 Corinthians 8: 9

"This verse isn't talking about spiritual poverty!" Pastor Richard was very emphatic. "Do you really think Jesus Christ was spiritually poor?"

Well, yes, actually, I do, I thought.

Jesus Christ left His throne in heaven, left His Father and His precious Holy Spirit, to voluntarily come down to earth to live here in this mess. In heaven, there was no lack. Jesus didn't have to call a three-way meeting of the Trinity to discuss anything. The three were one. Here on earth, the Spirit had to descend on Him at His baptism, and Jesus had to pray to His Father continually to receive His instructions. He went from limitless spiritual communion and oneness, to a solitary life, stuck in a limited human body.

Yes, I think Jesus voluntarily became spiritually poor, so that I could receive the riches of eternal life with God. But my pastors most emphatically disagreed.

One Sunday morning, the pastors announced after service that the church camera needed to be replaced. Our services were streamed live on many social media platforms, and the camera we were using was outdated and not of the best quality. Pastor Richard asked the congregation to pray about how much money each person could contribute toward a new camera. "Sister Amy will collect the money," he said confidently. "Just give your offerings to her, as you get them, and she will keep the money until we have enough."

As usual, this made me nervous. I had to think of a safe place to stash this money until the goal amount was reached. Everyone in the church seemed to prefer dealing with cash only. But I located a suitable spot, and started collecting. Pastor Richard had given a deadline of about a month to come up with the total amount due.

When the day arrived, he asked me how much we had collected. "Six hundred dollars," I replied. He frowned.

"That's not nearly enough," he said. I remained silent. He thought for a while, then told me to just deposit the money in the church account.

At our next Sunday service, he announced that we had not met our goal to purchase a new camera, and therefore, it would not be purchased at that time.

"And shame on all of you!" he finished, before sitting down.

I was stunned. The people who had given toward the camera had given in good faith. Now what?

At this same time, one of the young women in the church decided that she also wanted to take up a special offering, to buy the pastors a new car. Their old Chevrolet was on its last legs. So once again, I kept an envelope that was full of cash, and added to it every week.

I wondered what to tell the people who had contributed toward the camera that was never purchased. What if this happens all over again?

You don't have any faith, I scolded myself. *We will buy the pastors a new car. Just wait and see.*

After about six weeks, we had seven thousand dollars collected toward the car. This was not enough. Once again, in an after-church meeting, I was told to deposit the money in the church account.

This time, I felt I had to speak up. "What about the people who gave toward the camera, and the car?" I asked. "We ended up buying neither. Shouldn't they get their money back?"

After a moment of stunned silence, both pastors started talking at once. "Yes, of course," they said. "Yes, they should get their money back."

"Or, at least, just tell them that the money was put into the general fund, because we didn't reach our goal," I said lamely. My beloved pastors' expressions and shocked silence made me feel that my suggestion had been totally inappropriate.

Was I wrong? I tried to step back and look at the situation objectively. If a church member gave money toward a very specific cause, and that cause was not fulfilled, wouldn't he want to know about it? Wouldn't she want an explanation?

Nothing further was said about this, but that night, my phone started ringing.

"Hello, this is Francisca from church. I gave $700.00 toward the car, and I want my money back."

"Hello, this is Ms. Rodriguez. I would like my money back, please."

I made a note of every person who called, and the amount they were requesting, and compared it to my records. And then, at church the next day, Pastor Richard came into the office.

He sat down, and began speaking very quietly, so quietly that I could hardly hear him.

"You did not act in the right way," he said. "You stepped out of bounds by calling everyone and telling them they could get their money back."

"But I didn't!" I protested. I had called no one.

He went on as though he hadn't heard me. "This is causing division in the church. It is irresponsible. This is not the right way to handle this situation."

I explained, once again, that I had called no one in the church, and spoken to no one at all about returning their money. When I had left my meeting with the pastors, I had simply gone home, awaiting further instructions.

Pastor Richard went on, and on, and on. Nothing I said would convince him that I had not called anyone. He told me, again and again, what a grave error I had made, and what a serious mistake it was. He finally stood up.

"I hope we have learned something from this," he said, as he turned toward the door.

My frustration boiled over. "What have we learned?" I snapped. "I told you that I called no one! So, what have we learned?"

He looked at me a final time, then walked out of the room.

The next time I saw Pastor Leah, I made a beeline toward her. She had always been so kind to me. She had always listened to me and offered her wisdom. I knew she would help me.

"Pastor Leah!" I began, struggling to maintain my composure. "Pastor Richard thinks I called everyone and told them they could get their money back. But I didn't! I told him that, but he didn't believe me!"

Pastor Leah smiled her gentle smile at me, and said nothing. I looked at her, and she smiled at me, and there was silence.

What is happening here? Maybe she doesn't feel comfortable talking about her husband when he's not here.

As she continued smiling at me, I knew. She was the one who had called everyone, and she had not told her husband that she'd done that. And from her silence, I knew that she wasn't going to, either.

This was one of many instances that occurred in the church where I realized that the communication between my two pastors was very minimal. I believe this lack of communication then trickled down to the congregation. While I certainly don't need to know everything that is going on in the church, and I certainly don't want to stick my nose into other people's business, there are some things that I definitely do need to know about.

This incident was very hurtful to me. I felt unheard and un-believed, and didn't appreciate being made the fall guy in a marital miscommunication. I also knew that I had to forgive both of them, and I did.

I knew that I had probably crossed a line by criticizing how these financial issues had been handled. I had heard so many times about how God would punish those who criticized the ministry. I was waiting for the ax to fall.

***

One evening after our Bible study, Pastor Leah stopped me after the service. "Can I talk to you for a minute?" she asked. "I wanted to let you know of our upcoming travel plans," she said with a big smile. "We are going on a missions' trip to Honduras. While we are there, we plan to stop off and visit some relatives in Guatemala."

"Oh, that sounds great!" I said enthusiastically. "What an opportunity!"

She nodded. "Yes, a church we know there has invited us to come. There are going to be hundreds of people there. We believe God is going to touch so many, and people will be saved."

I was excited to hear this. We put our heads together and began to plan for the time that they would be gone. They would be taking the media team, and Cheri would be going along to look after their children while they were ministering.

I blinked. *Wow,* I thought. *I wonder how much all of this is going to cost? Plane tickets for that many people? Hotel rooms?*

Pastor Leah read my thoughts. Both she and Pastor Richard had a habit of doing that.

"I wanted to ask you," she began hesitantly. "Can you get me a secured credit card?"

I was puzzled. "What is a secured credit card?" I had never heard that term before.

"It's a card that has both your name and my name on it," she explained.

Oh. She wanted me to co-sign a credit card for her. I looked down at the floor, not knowing what to say.

"There are going to be churches attending this conference from all of the surrounding area," Pastor Leah went on. "They are going to take up an offering for us every evening. Whatever travel charges we put on the credit card, we will be able to pay back right away."

Well, that did a lot to alleviate my concerns. This was a wonderful opportunity to reach lost souls, and bring them into the kingdom of God. We couldn't pass this up.

I set aside my doubts regarding co-signing. Pastor Leah knew the Bible better than I did. If she was asking me to do this, it couldn't be wrong, could it?

Oh, yes indeed, it could.

A man void of understanding striketh hands, and becometh surety in the presence of his friend. Proverbs 17: 18

I applied for the credit card, was approved, and the ministry group set off for Honduras. I was the stand-in preacher while they were gone, and the church prayed for them every day.

A few days before they were due back, I got a phone call from Pastor Richard. He wanted to know what our bank's international routing number was, so the Honduras church could deposit money directly into the church's account. This sounded very exciting to me, and I checked the bank every day, eager to see how much money would be coming in.

Instead of a huge influx of cash, I saw the account go negative. This greatly alarmed me, and I texted both pastors, asking what was going on. They were traveling and running between flights with their phones on airplane mode, and I didn't hear from them until they were back in the United States.

At our Tuesday prayer meeting, they arrived looking travel-worn and exhausted. Pastor Richard was his usual upbeat self. Pastor Leah was subdued and mostly silent. As the service was winding down, Pastor Leah pulled me aside.

"The woman who was hosting us gathered the offering every night," she said. "We just assumed she would give it to us before we left. Finally we asked her about it, and she said she needed that money to pay for the food, the hotel, the conference room rental, and everything else. We got nothing. Nothing. She took all of the offerings."

I sat in stunned silence. How could this be possible? How could a fellow Christian treat visiting pastors like this?

"She will pay for this," I said, finally. "God will discipline her." I could think of nothing positive to say. I was crushed and horrified.

"Many people came to Christ," Pastor Leah managed a sad smile. "Many souls were saved. That is the work of God. That is what we have to focus on."

What is the price of a human soul? I wondered. *Can we calculate its value? How much are souls worth?*

Twenty-six thousand dollars, it turns out. That is the amount I saw when I pulled up the online credit card statement.

For weeks after this, I walked around in a daze. I alternated between being furiously angry, and crying uncontrollably. I simply could not understand the level of deception involved in tricking two of God's servants into traveling thousands of miles, under the guise of holding a church conference, while having no intention of ever paying them a dime for their ministry. How does that even happen? How could someone be so wicked?

My mind went off on many tangents. I wondered how I, too, could fleece other people out of thousands of dollars, thereby recouping my losses. Drug dealing? Prostitution? Extortion? Arms smuggling?

We never really spoke about this incident again. After all, what was there to say? When I checked the credit card online, I saw that monthly payments were being made. The interest charged on the balance due was far greater than the payments being made.

After about a year, Pastor Leah mentioned in passing that she had 'let the card go.' I did not understand what she meant by that, and was afraid to ask. But I didn't need to, because in a few days' time I got a letter from the bank.

"Your line of credit has been canceled due to non-payment of outstanding debt. Your credit card number –XXX4 has been canceled."

Online, I pulled up the credit card I had co-signed for Pastor Leah. The bank had written it off as a bad debt. My credit rating, once in the eight hundred range, had plummeted to the four hundred range.

I felt sick to my stomach.

Something had happened in my subconscious mind at that point, something that I was consciously unaware of. A door was beginning to close, very slowly.

***

Guadalupe seemed to have disappeared from the planet. The texts I sent her went unanswered, and the voice mails I left her went unreturned. One day, while feeling particularly down, I called her, crying, and left a pitiful voicemail.

"Guadalupe, where are you? I miss you so much. There are so many things I want to talk to you about. If I have done anything to hurt you, I'm sorry! Can we please just talk?"

A few months later, Pastor Richard asked to speak with me after service.

"We are building a house in Guatemala," he announced. I was amazed, and sat there with my mouth open.

"Why?" I finally asked. "Are you moving back?"

He smiled. "No," he said. "We just want to have a place to go to visit – kind of a refuge. Also, a place to host other pastors when they come to visit."

I waited in silence. *How can they afford to build a house in Guatemala?* I knew the ongoing financial problems the church had always had.

"Building a house over there is a lot different than building one here," Pastor Richard said. "It's much, much cheaper."

I continued to wait. I knew what was coming.

"The builders contacted us yesterday," he went on. "They can't go any further until they get ten thousand dollars. Can you help?"

I thought I had heard him incorrectly. *You are asking me to give you ten thousand dollars, when you defaulted on our joint credit card, and ruined my credit rating?*

Pastor Leah had told me earlier that she would pay off the credit card, even though the bank had written it off. "You know what kind of people we are," she'd said. "We don't cheat people. We don't leave our bills unpaid."

I wanted to get up and run out of the room, away from Pastor Richard and his request. I resolved, this time, to stare him down. I looked him full in the eyes for a few seconds and never broke my gaze. I finally said, "I don't have ten thousand dollars. The best I can do is five thousand."

I did have five thousand dollars in my savings account, and withdrawing it would leave me with about two bucks. Why did I offer it? I don't really know.

"Yes, that will help," Pastor Richard smiled at me. I opened my purse and wrote a check, asking him to not cash it until I had time to transfer the money.

That night, I lay in bed, restless and unable to sleep. Thoughts kept forcing themselves into my mind, and I kept trying to thrust them out.

How much money have you given to this church over the years? What do you, and what does the church, have to show for it?

I couldn't answer that question. The truth was, I probably would never know the answer to that question, here on earth.

I had given, not hundreds, but thousands of dollars to the church. I had given my ten percent tithe, which in my mind was a requirement of being a Christian, and I had given thousands on top of that.

Lay not up for yourselves treasures upon earth, where moth and rust doth corrupt, and where thieves break through and steal: But lay up for yourselves treasures in heaven, where neither moth nor rust doth corrupt, and where thieves do not break through nor steal: For where your treasure is, there will your heart be also. Matthew 6: 19 - 21

Where is my treasure? I wondered. *Where is my heart?*

I loved my pastors, and I loved my church friends with all of my being. Yes, there had been misunderstandings and hurt feelings along the way, but that is true of every family. These people truly were my family. Other than my sister, I felt closer to my church than my own biological relatives. But why the constant financial pressure? What was really going on?

I just didn't know.

Was it really necessary to build a house in Guatemala? Honestly, it seemed absolutely crazy to me that they would even think of doing that. Maybe they really did have plans to move back there, and just didn't want to discuss it with me. After all, where they live is their own business.

But why do I have to finance their business? I thought crossly.

There were so many times that Pastor Leah hadn't been able to make payroll or pay payroll taxes for her first business, and I had deposited my own money in her business account. I did this because I couldn't stand to see her employees working without pay. But the second business, in my opinion, was a lost cause. I never put a dime into that one.

I wondered if I would be somehow legally liable if I knew about a business that was in essence employing slave labor! Everything was such a mess.

God, You are going to have to take care of this somehow, I prayed.

Then I fell asleep.

Chapter 4: The lies

Guadalupe's words popped into my mind at the oddest times.

Sometimes, when people think about faith, they can't tell the difference between faith and fantasy.

I had read accounts of people being raised from the dead. I had known, in person, someone who had stage four cancer and was healed instantaneously, causing the oncologist to have a nervous breakdown.

In my own life, I had a pending court case that looked as though I was about to lose everything I owned, only to have the person who was suing me not show up in court on the appointed day.

And there are a hundred other examples I could give of God stepping in and doing something impossible. Every example is a result of faith!

One thing I had learned from my beloved pastors, over and over, was to have unwavering faith in God. Rather than pray a little prayer, then discard it when things didn't turn out as I wanted, they had taught me to pray without ceasing, and to not give up.

But my pastors were not angelic beings. They were, and are, simply human beings. And all human beings are flawed.

"Job did not understand his situation!" Pastor Richard was preaching one Sunday morning. "He did not understand that he had a devil fighting him. When he said, *"...the LORD gave, and the LORD hath taken away; blessed be the name of the LORD* (Job 1: 21b)" he was saying that every bad thing that happened to him was God's doing!"

Well, it was *God's doing,* I thought obstinately. Pastor Richard went on.

"People love to sing this so-called 'Christian' song," he said.

He gives and takes away,
He gives and takes away,
My heart will choose to say,
Lord, blessed be Your Name.

"The Lord doesn't take away anything! The Bible says the blessings of God maketh rich, and He addeth no sorrow with it (Proverbs 10: 22)."

This was one of Pastor Richard's favorite verses, and he quoted it often.

It made no sense to me. In the last chapter of the book of Job, we read that his friends and family came to visit Job, for this reason:

...and they bemoaned him, and comforted him over all the evil that the LORD had brought upon him: Job 42: 11b

Pastor Richard and Leah had lost their third child to miscarriage! Isn't God the one who gives the gift of children?

Lo, children are an heritage of the LORD: and the fruit of the womb is his reward. Psalm 127: 3

How could the Lord give a child, then take her away, if He never takes anything away?

See now that I, even I, am he, and there is no god with me: I kill, and I make alive; I wound, and I heal: neither is there any that can deliver out of my hand. Deuteronomy 32: 39

I form the light, and create darkness: I make peace, and create evil: I the LORD do all these things. Isaiah 45: 7

True, I had a much more negative outlook on life than my pastors had. No matter what had happened to them, they always seemed to find the silver lining. But I was beginning to think that the church was crossing over from faith into fantasy.

"Though He slay me, yet will I praise Him," Pastor Richard went on.

"Trust," I said out loud, before I could stop myself.

"Excuse me?" Pastor Richard stopped his sermon and looked at me.

Oh, why can't I keep my mouth shut? I berated myself.

"It's trust, not praise," I said quietly.

Though He slay me, yet will I trust in him (Job 13: 15).

"Trust, praise, it's the same thing," he said impatiently, and went on.

No, it's not the same thing, at all, I thought.

There was so much of that at Boundless Horizons church. Both pastors often misquoted Romans 4: 17b.

...even God, who quickeneth the dead, and calleth those things which be not as though they were.

They quoted this verse as: Faith calls the things that are not, as though they are.

So many times Pastor Leah said to the congregation, "If only you could see what I'm seeing! Just believe! God is only asking you to believe!"

I knew I didn't have the 'crazy faith' that Pastor Leah had, but I wanted it. Oh, how I wanted it.

One day, my doorbell rang out of the blue. There, on my front step, was Guadalupe.

"Guadalupe!" I was so overjoyed I almost knocked her over with my hug. "Where have you been? I've missed you so much! Come in, come in!"

Guadalupe came in. She was dressed in shorts and a tank top. I was so used to seeing her in elegant, floor-length dresses that I hardly recognized her.

"I can't stay long," she began, grinning. "I just wanted to let you know that I am moving to Washington, D.C."

I felt the air go out of me like a pricked balloon. "Washington? What on earth? No, you can't move so far away!"

"My sister got a fantastic job offer that she couldn't turn down, and I'm going with her," she said. I kept staring at her. Surely, this was some kind of mistake.

"The truck is loaded and parked outside," she went on. "I've got to hit the road!"

I peeked through the window, and sure enough, there was the moving truck. 'You're moving today – right now?!" I gasped.

"It's a great opportunity for us," she smiled.

I had too many questions. "I've been trying to get ahold of you for months!" I exclaimed. "You didn't reply to any of my messages."

"Oh, that," she waved her hand. "I've been really busy. I'll text you when I get there, and give you my new address. Gotta go – 'bye!"

And in an instant, she was gone.

I sat down heavily. My head was spinning. What on earth?

Obviously, my friendship with Guadalupe was much more one-sided than I had thought. *That's okay,* I tried to remind myself. *How many times have other people wanted to be your friend, and you were the one who just wasn't that interested?*

But I had honestly thought that Guadalupe and I were much closer than we actually were. I'd thought of her as another sister. I loved her deeply. And now, she was gone.

Weeks went by, and the text from Guadalupe never came. Her social media accounts were set up in such a way that I couldn't message her. As before, my texts and voicemails to her went unanswered.

My grief turned into rage. If she didn't want to be my friend any more, why carry out the charade of stopping at my house and telling me she was moving?

I hadn't heard from her for months before she landed on my doorstep. Why not just get in your stupid truck and leave town? Why drag me into this emotional vortex?

As seemed to be the case a lot lately, I had a lot of questions, and I had no answers.

***

Pastor Leah called me at work one day. "Can you come over to the church?" she asked. "We are filming a TV commercial for the ministry," she said.

"But, I'm at work," I protested. "I don't think I can just leave with no notice."

"Yes, you can," she said encouragingly. "It will be fine; don't worry."

I was actually very worried about this, but I sent my boss a quick email about having to take care of something, clocked out, and left. As I drove to the church, I was filled with anxiety.

I can't just leave in the middle of the day without requesting it in advance, I stewed. *What if I get fired? Oh, God, please don't let me get fired.*

When I arrived at the church, there were two other church members there. A camera man had set up some lights and a huge camera. He was interviewing one of the members, and filming his answers. The questions were all about the church, the ministry, and how it had affected his life.

Then it was my turn. I gave a brief testimony about my life and what it had been like before I started attending Boundless Horizons. I talked about the love and camaraderie we all felt in church. I had to remind myself to keep smiling – no one who saw the commercial would want to attend our church if she felt it was full of gloomy people.

After about an hour and a half, the filming was over, and I raced out the door. I did not get fired, but, the commercial never aired on TV. I wondered if the camera man had even been from our local TV station. I wondered if there was some other purpose, completely unknown to me, behind the filmed question and answer sessions.

The commercial was never mentioned again, by anyone.

***

"At the end of service today, it's going to start to rain," Pastor Leah announced. "This will be a sign from God."

It didn't start to rain.

A tearful Pastor Leah told me after service one Sunday that their water was about to be shut off, because they hadn't paid the bill. Early Monday morning I called the water company and asked to pay it. I was told it was paid in full.

I stood in my home, perplexed. My home. I looked around. The house that I had purchased, at Pastor Leah's direction, because if I did, she said, the one thing that I had been praying for and longing for, for so many years, would finally come to me.

It didn't.

Later, a guest preacher, hand-picked by the pastors, was going down the prayer line, laying hands on people and praying for them. Each person fell over backwards, "slain in the Spirit," as we were told. When he got to me, he pushed on my forehead so hard that I fell backwards.

I now knew the secret. If you push on someone hard enough, she will definitely fall down.

Another guest preacher, who had come and gone, started yelling at me over the phone about how Pastor Richard would not return any of his phone calls. When I asked Pastor Richard about this, I was told that the guest preacher was a racist, so he didn't want to talk to him.

Pastor Leah's second business was failing badly. She needed an infusion of cash. She approached one of the single mothers in the church and asked for a loan. The woman turned her down, and promptly left the church. She then asked a married couple in the church, and they refused, and also left the church. She asked the ex-boyfriend of one of the young women in the church, someone she hardly knew, to lend her the money. He became so angry that he didn't talk to his ex for over a month, someone he had previously been on good terms with. Then she came to me. I almost started laughing hysterically, but instead, I managed to say no. She then went to my sister, who had been a long-time online supporter of the ministry, and my sister gave her several thousand dollars.

"I promise I will pay you back!" Pastor Leah vowed.

She didn't.

***

I was really missing Guadalupe. My anger toward her had dissolved into just a simple sadness. One day, I mentioned it to Pastor Leah.

"I know she had to move to Washington for her sister's job," I said sadly. "I just wish she would let me know how she's doing."

"Guadalupe is in Kentucky," Pastor Leah said firmly. "She's not in Washington. She never went to Washington."

"Whaaaat? Why did she tell me she was moving to Washington?" I was dumbfounded.

Pastor Leah shrugged her shoulders. "Who knows?" she said.

I felt a red flag rising. "How do you know she's in Kentucky?" I asked, suspiciously.

"I called my minister friend there, and as we were talking on the phone, she told me that Guadalupe was there, attending her church," Pastor Leah explained.

None of this made any sense. Why drop in out of nowhere to tell me you're leaving the state, and then lie to me about where you're going? What was the purpose of all this?

Guadalupe, do you really hate me that much? What did I ever do to you?

Later, I questioned both stories. Guadalupe was probably not in Washington, nor in Kentucky. She was probably in Yemen, doing missionary work. The story that I made up in my mind about her made as much sense as any other story I had heard. How was I to know what was fact and what was fiction? Maybe everything was fiction. Maybe there really was no person named Guadalupe who had been my friend. Maybe I had simply conjured her up, out of loneliness.

I knew I was being ridiculous, but I felt like the very core of my life was becoming ridiculous.

The next time I saw my sister, I apologized to her for introducing her to my pastors. She stared at me in astonishment. I was so embarrassed that I couldn't look at her.

"If I hadn't introduced to you Pastor Leah, she would not have asked to borrow money from you. I feel like it's all my fault. You'll never get that money back!" I felt like crying.

Angela looked at me tenderly. "This is a lesson I had to learn," she said softly. "God will take care of the situation. Don't worry about it."

We hugged, and I thanked God, as I had done many times, for my sister.

Chapter 5: The awakening

Pastor Leah's businesses began a breathtaking downward spiral. I had never seen anything decline so rapidly. It was very painful to watch.

At Tuesday night prayer meetings, she prayed for her businesses, prayed for new clients, prayed for cash to come in. We all joined with her in these prayers. We had all heard Pastor Leah say, many times, that God had told her to start these businesses, so if He had, how could they fail?

Everything about both businesses was picture perfect. The offices, the logos (which Pastor Leah had designed herself), the furniture, the advertising – everything was spot on. Yet the numbers of clients and customers continued to decline.

Cheri had told me that originally, she and Pastor Leah had been equal partners in the first business. Then, Pastor Leah had asked her to sign over her portion of the business completely to her. Cheri had been hurt by this at first, but then came to realize that it was a blessing in disguise. Cheri had gotten off the sinking ship before it went down with her on it.

As usual, I was simply confused. Pastor Leah had told me that Cheri had come to her and told her that she wanted to sign her part of the business over to her. The two stories were complete opposites. They couldn't both be true!

It was one more example of the extreme lack of communication in the ministry, from the leadership, and in the businesses that Pastor Leah managed.

As bookkeeper for both businesses, it was my responsibility to gather up the receipts, the paid bills, and the deposits, and enter them on the computer. For some reason I could never put my finger on, I dreaded going into the office. I felt a dark cloud come over me every time I went there. I didn't know why!

Pastor Leah had had a horrible experience with a potential employee who had attempted to steal client records from the office. This was a person who hadn't even been given a key, yet somehow found a way to get in and rifle through all the drawers. I had still been in the very beginning process of bringing a new employee into the company - calling her references. No offer of employment had even been extended yet. Then Pastor Leah called me early one morning.

"It seems as though someone has been in the office overnight," she began. "Was it you?"

"No, I replied," very alarmed. "What's going on?"

"Someone pulled all the files out of the file cabinets, and threw them on the floor. The toner has been taken out of the copy machine and dumped on the floor, also."

"What? Oh my God! You need to call the police!" I shrieked into the phone.

"No," she said quietly. "I know who did this. It was Natalie. I am going to change the locks."

But how on earth did Natalie get in, if she didn't have a key? After calling all of her references, I came to the conclusion that Natalie was a professional criminal, and I was baffled as to why she listed people as references who had such horrible things to say about her, such as:

"She's a thief. She stole money from our organization."

"She stole client files, then stole the clients!"

"Natalie called the police and reported that we were using drugs on the job, and none of us were."

And, my favorite (and the most chilling): "I don't usually give references because I don't want the legal liability, but this woman is pure evil, and she needs to be stopped."

We changed the locks, and Natalie disappeared somewhere into the darkness. But as the months went on, I sometimes wondered if she had placed a curse on Pastor Leah's businesses.

Pastor Leah had recounted to me that, right before the break-in, she was supposed to meet Natalie for a second interview. She arrived at the office to find Natalie burning incense outside the door, and chanting something under her breath.

Pure evil. And now, both businesses were hanging by a thread.

I knew, in my heart, that the cash that my sister had invested into the businesses would never be repaid. It also seemed quite obvious to me that Pastor Leah would never discuss the unpaid debt. It was painful.

One ordinary spring day, when everything seemed as normal as it could possibly be, Pastor Leah made an announcement at our Thursday evening Bible study.

"We are moving to Arizona," she said, as though it was a matter of no consequence.

There was a shocked silence in the room. Everyone stared at her. She went on.

"The Lord told me two years ago that we needed to move, but I resisted. I can't disobey Him any longer. We will be moving soon."

This bombshell announcement seemed to cover everyone with shock, silence, fear and grief, all at the same time. No one knew what to say.

"We have never been accepted in the community," Pastor Leah said. "People have fought us at every turn. People have spread lies about us, to the point that the businesses lost customers. It's time for us to start fresh somewhere else."

My head was spinning. If God told them to leave their home in Guatemala and come here, if God told them to start a ministry here, and start businesses here, what had happened? Did God change His mind?

You could argue that the businesses and the ministry had not been covered in prayer, and that's why they failed, but that is absolutely not true in this case. We bathed everything in prayer, all the time.

Was this simply a test? Was God drying up the ministry and the businesses, as a way of testing the pastors' faith?

My pastors had more faith than any people I had ever met, ever, in my life. But human beings do have their limits. When there is no food on the table, and no shoes on your child's feet, your faith has been stretched to the breaking point.

Once again, I felt extreme anger at some of the congregation. A tiny handful of us tithed – the rest didn't. *If everyone had tithed, as the Bible tells us to do, this wouldn't have happened!* I raged inwardly. How many times had I talked to the congregation about tithing? Too many to count. I was always met with a sea of blank faces; indeed, whenever I spoke about it, some people had even appeared to be asleep.

My pastors had always tithed on whatever tiny amount they had gotten from the church, to a nationally-known ministry. The Bible says that if you tithe, God will open the windows of heaven and pour out blessings on you (Malachi 3: 10). Why hadn't that happened in their case?

We don't give our tithes and offerings, hoping to get something back. We give because God expects us to give. I had always believed in and practiced tithing as if it was a given – you could no more not tithe than you could not breathe. I had seen my pastors give when they really had nothing to give, time and time again. Yet Malachi 3:10 did not seem to apply in their lives. Why not? I didn't have the answer to that question.

We all began preparing for the move, and there was a lot to do.

One by one, the young women in the church stated that they, too, would move to Arizona. All of these young ladies were single and working jobs that could easily be done in any state. Pastor Leah asked each one if she was sure that was what she wanted to do, and each one replied with an excited yes. When the dust settled, there were a small minority of people who elected not to move. Most had children in school, except for me. I just didn't want to move.

And, I also think that subconsciously, I saw this as a way to escape. If so, it was buried very deeply in my subconscious mind, because my conscious mind was shocked and grieved at the thought of losing my beloved friends.

Nights were spent at the church, boxing up everything. Pastor Leah brought over her unsold inventory from her second business, boxed it up, and put it in the church storage room. The overhead lights were unscrewed from the ceiling and boxed up. The curtains behind the podium were taken down and boxed up.

I participated in all of this, but felt strangely numb as I worked alongside everyone else. I didn't understand the logic involved. Why take the lights and the curtains? The pastors had no location in mind in Arizona for a new church building. There was no place to put all this stuff.

Our rented church space in the strip mall was soon crowded with hundreds of boxes. As I stood back and surveyed the disarray, once again, faith and fantasy collided.

They are going to need a semi-truck to move all this stuff, I thought. *And when they get there, where will they put it?*

I mentioned my concerns to Pastor Leah.

"I found someone who will drive a semi to Arizona for us, for three thousand dollars," she said confidently.

"What?!" I exclaimed. "That's not possible."

"That's the price he quoted me," she said. "We just have to tell him the day, and he will be here."

I looked at my beloved pastor with a mixture of love and irritation. Pastor Leah always sees the good in everyone, and always takes people at face value. Despite having been tricked and betrayed many times, she simply believes what people tell her. I knew this truck deal was a scam, but decided to keep quiet for the moment.

We continued packing, getting more boxes, packing some more, donating stuff, and packing some more. Everyone reported to the church every night of the week, and just started working.

Pastor Leah was very busy packing up her own house, so she couldn't always join us. How I wanted to simply throw away so many of the things we were packing up! But it wasn't my decision to make.

Pastor Leah spent many hours online, looking for affordable housing. She found a very nice house for her family, and nice apartments for the young women to share. I saw pictures of them online; they all seemed too good to be true.

The church advertised many items for sale on social media, but there were few sales. Pastor Leah had priced everything very high. I tried explaining to her that when people go to a moving sale, they are expecting moving sale prices. The prices she had put on many of the items was the same as what a brand-new item was. We had a lot of lookers, but few takers.

At one point, both pastors pulled me aside for a meeting.

"We have talked to the landlord," Pastor Richard said. "He has agreed to let us store some things here until we can find a place to put them in Arizona."

"Wow," I said. "That's very nice of him."

"Yes, he's a good man," Pastor Richard agreed.

As always, my natural tendency was to rush in and grab every situation by the horns, but something (I believe the Holy Spirit) told me to stay out of the decisions that were being made, as much as possible.

All of it still seemed like a dream. I thought I would wake up and find out that no one was moving to Arizona, and everything would go on exactly as it had before.

There were so many delays and setbacks regarding the move. Time dragged on and on. The plan had been to move at the end of the school year, in the spring, get settled in the new community, and enroll the children in their new schools in August. But nothing seemed to be working out.

Pastor Leah texted me and asked if I would co-sign on a house lease for them in Arizona. After the fiasco of the joint credit card, I was shocked that she asked. Somehow, I found the strength to say no. She replied that she understood, and it was okay.

Am I the only one in this church who has a job? I thought angrily. *Am I the only one who saves money in a savings account? Why have I become a bank to these people?*

I had resigned myself to the fact of everyone moving – so much so that I was almost impatient for them to go. In a way I was like a wounded animal, thinking: *Just go away and leave me alone.*

After yet another setback, I met with the pastors again. Pastor Leah was sobbing.

"Am I such a terrible sinner, that God will not answer my prayers?" she wept. Pastor Richard sat silently, with a stone face. "God told us to go. But there has been one problem after another." She sobbed and sobbed, tears pouring down her face.

I absolutely couldn't stand this. Pastor Leah was one of my dearest friends. Before I knew what I was saying, I offered to give them five thousand dollars to pay the deposit and first month's rent on their house. It was as though someone else was saying the words, but they were coming out of my mouth.

Why did you say that? I was horrified at myself. But I had said it, and I couldn't take it back.

I guess I thought that the sooner they left, the sooner I could retreat into my corner, lick my wounds, and try to rebuild my life. It's nothing to be proud of, but it's how I felt at the time.

Strangely, Pastor Leah went on sobbing as though she hadn't heard me, yet I know she had. She continued to sob and sob. I realized then just how stressful the potential move was to her, and the enormous toll it had taken on her. Pastor Richard continued to sit in silence.

Finally, he said, "I look at my children and I wonder what I will have to leave them? I have nothing to leave them. I have no inheritance for them."

I was determined not to let my irritation show. *You would have an inheritance for them, if you would get a job,* I thought. But I didn't say it out loud.

Awkwardly, I reached into my purse and pulled out my checkbook. I wrote the check in Pastor Richard's name, and handed it to him. He looked at me with tears in his eyes, but said nothing. I offered to pray for them both, and they nodded.

I prayed that God would strengthen them, provide for them, guide them, and protect them.

The atmosphere in the room was subdued. It was as though they didn't want to move, and no one in the church wanted them to move, but everyone knew they had to move. It was an odd situation.

Once again, my savings account had been drained down to zero. I felt rather numb about this. After all, they had not asked me for money this time; I had just volunteered to give it to them.

After that, things began moving quickly. We all met at the pastors' house one night to load up the truck. As I pulled up in my car, I saw a small box truck.

"What happened to the semi?" I asked. Pastor Leah said that the semi-truck rental had turned out to be a scam. Of course, I had known this when she first mentioned it to me, but nevertheless it was still disappointing.

I found Pastor Richard loading boxes in the truck. There was a chain of people passing boxes from the house to the garage, to the truck. I could see immediately that the truck was way too small to hold everything.

"After we're done here, we'll drive over to the church and start loading up all the boxes there," Pastor Richard declared.

"But they won't fit," I said, puzzled.

"My faith tells me that they will fit." He fixed me with a steely gaze.

How could I argue with that?

We worked and worked. The mood was somber.

During a brief break to wipe the sweat off my face, I offered to clean the pastors' house after it was empty. Pastor Leah was horrified.

"Oh, no," she said. "That would be too much for you. We can't ask you to do that."

I smiled at my dear friend. "You haven't asked me – I've offered!" I said. "Really, it's no big deal."

"Are you sure?" she asked doubtfully.

"Of course. I want you to get your deposit back."

At midnight, the truck was still being loaded. There was approximately two feet of space left to fill up. I looked at the mountains of boxes, at the huge couch sectional, the tables, and the lamps, and knew that almost all of it would have to be left behind. It went without saying that nothing from the church could be loaded in that truck.

I was bone weary, and even though I felt a little guilty, I said goodnight. They were almost done, anyway.

The next day, I learned that they had not left at the crack of dawn, as I had assumed they would. After work, I headed over there again.

The pastors, their children, the young women from church, and several neighbors were all gathered in the driveway. Everyone was saying goodbye and taking pictures. The young women had packed their own vehicles full of their possessions, and they were all going to caravan together. This made me very uneasy. It was a fourteen-hour drive, and they were planning on driving all night. It's definitely something I would not do!

I hugged everyone as the tears poured down my face. I loved these people so much! They had been my whole life for the past eleven years. I was closer to them than my own family. Would I ever see them again? We were all crying.

I watched everyone get into their various vehicles, clutching the keys to the pastors' house in my hand. I watched them drive away.

For eleven years I had served under these people. They, and the young women in the church, were my closest friends. They were my life.

Is this how the disciples felt when Jesus ascended up into heaven? Frightened, abandoned, contemplating an unknown future, not having any idea of how to live on Earth without Him?

I didn't know, but somehow, I would have to figure it all out.

Chapter 6: The revelations

I threw myself into cleaning the pastors' house.

The enormous couch sectional still filled the driveway, so I parked on the street. I had received a hasty text from Pastor Leah while they were on the road, instructing me to donate or throw away whatever was left behind. She also told me that they had sold their land and unfinished house in Guatemala, to help finance their move.

The house I gave you five thousand dollars to build? I asked myself silently. Yep, that was the one.

I eyed the sectional filling the driveway. How was I to donate or throw away that monstrous piece of furniture? I couldn't with my little car. I decided to leave it for now.

I unlocked the door and went in. Boxes and boxes of items left behind greeted me. *Well, she told me to donate them, so I will,* I thought.

Food, kitchen items, personal items, children's toys…it was overwhelming. I opened a kitchen drawer to discover that it was stuffed full of old receipts and bills. Most of the bills were marked "Past Due" or "Final Notice." I shouldn't have been surprised, but I was.

"You know what kind of people we are," Pastor Leah had said earlier. "We don't cheat people. We don't leave our bills unpaid."

Well, it was obvious to me that they did leave their bills unpaid.

It's painful to say this, but I was frankly shocked at the condition of the house. The carpet was filthy and the walls had food encrusted on them, in almost every room of the house. It looked as though someone had thrown a bowl of gravy at the wall in one spot, and a bowl of barbeque sauce in another. The bathrooms were filthy. The master bathroom looked as though it had not been cleaned in years.

Yes, I was shocked. A dawning realization was coming over me, and I didn't like it.

Pastor Richard had always been a stay-at-home dad, while Pastor Leah had run her businesses and tried to bring money into the family. I had always known that there was a tremendous burden on her shoulders. Based on the condition of the house, I began to believe that Pastor Leah had been suffering from depression for quite some time.

She would never say this out loud, of course. I thought back to the times I had learned she had been hospitalized, always after the fact. This had continually baffled me. Didn't she want us to pray for her? Didn't she want us to visit her in the hospital?

Maybe I hadn't gotten all the facts regarding her hospitalizations. Maybe there was more to the story.

Looking around the filthy house, I felt extreme anger toward Pastor Richard. Each couple has to manage their own family life in a way that works for them, but come on! If his wife was the breadwinner, couldn't he scrub out the shower once in a while?

I had always felt closer to Pastor Leah than Pastor Richard, probably because she is a woman and I could relate better to her. But now I felt a huge chasm opening up between me and him. I felt that he had abdicated his responsibility toward his wife and family. I was mad.

Pastor Leah's bra and robe were on the hook on the bathroom door. Her hair products and makeup were on the counter. She had just walked off and left it all.

I angrily grabbed some boxes and started throwing things in them. I made two sections on the living room floor for "donations" and "discard." My goal was to empty out the house first, then start scrubbing it. I had my work cut out for me.

It took about two weeks to clear out the house and clean it. The carpet was a lost cause; there was nothing that could be done about that. Someone had spilled red fruit juice on it, and no amount of carpet shampoo would eradicate that.

The kitchen sink drain was completely blocked and filled with foul-smelling water. I couldn't fix that, either.

I began to realize that there was no way on God's green earth that my pastors would get their deposit back. In fact, I was sure they would be on the hook to pay their landlord for damages.

Pastor Leah texted me that the landlord had contacted her, very angrily, about all the furniture left in the driveway. I just shook my head. What could I do about it? I had done everything I could with my little car.

Even when something really negative happens, some good can come out of it. Pastor Leah had left behind shelf after shelf of cleaning products, which, after I had thoroughly scrubbed the house, I donated. To myself.

***

I began receiving texts from the young women in the church. They had run into numerous obstacles in Arizona. Number one, they were not able to find affordable housing. The original apartment that they had put a deposit on was infested with cockroaches. Even though four of them had planned to share a place, they couldn't find anything else reasonably priced. Number two, no one could find steady jobs. A few of them had found part-time jobs, working a few hours here and there, but nothing that would be enough for rent and food. Everyone was staying with the pastors at the moment.

I remembered the pictures that Pastor Leah had shown me of their new rental house. It was huge. There was certainly room for everyone there; at least they would not be homeless.

All of this weighed heavily on me. If God had told the young women to go, why did He not provide for them?

By faith Abraham, when he was called to go out into a place which he should after receive for an inheritance, obeyed; and he went out, not knowing whither he went. Hebrews 11: 8

Everyone had stepped out in faith, and things were not going well. What was really happening here?

How were the pastors getting money? How were they paying rent? How were they buying food for their children?

After an online search, I found a non-profit organization about twenty minutes away from where they were living, and I sent the link to Pastor Leah. This non-profit provided food, utility payments, clothing and gas vouchers to the needy. Pastor Leah was very appreciative.

As for me, I was feeling more and more uneasy. The Bible says that if you minister the gospel, you should be paid from the gospel (1 Corinthians 9: 14). But what if the gospel is not paying you? Do you then just starve?

Pastor Richard had said, more times than I could count, that money was very easy to get, and he could simply snap his fingers and earn money. I wondered why he didn't.

But if any provide not for his own, and specially for those of his own house, he hath denied the faith, and is worse than an infidel. 1 Timothy 5: 8

No one wants to give up! Especially as a Christian, if God has told you to do something, you can't simply try for a while, then stop if it doesn't work out the way you thought it would. But my concerns about Pastor Richard were off the charts at this point.

For even when we were with you, this we commanded you, that if any would not work, neither should he eat. 2 Thessalonians 3: 10

***

I got a text from Cheri one day out of the blue.

I'm in town; can I stop by your work and talk to you for a little while?

I stared at my phone. She was back? What was going on?

I soon found out. Cheri had driven back, across three states, and was staying at her mom's house about seventy miles from where I lived. She had been unable to find work, and her bills were piling up. She had been re-hired at her old job, and was working steadily.

"I just need to get caught up on my bills," she sighed. "It's been so stressful in Arizona! I was afraid my car would get repossessed."

"Are you going back there?" I asked. I was stunned.

"Oh, yes," she assured me. "When I get caught up on my bills, I'll go back."

I asked her about the other girls. Nina hadn't been able to find work in her field, so was working part-time at a call center. Hannah was also working part-time. Faith had found a full time job and worked for several weeks, then had been laid off. Everyone was really hurting for money.

"What about the pastors?" I asked. "Are they surviving financially?"

"I don't ask," she said firmly. "God told them to move there, so I know He will take care of them."

"Will He?" I questioned. Oops. I had just said the quiet part out loud.

Cheri looked down at the floor. "I don't know what's going to happen," she said sadly. "Nothing has worked out for any of us."

We talked for quite a while. I was so happy to see her again, while simultaneously being sorry that she was going through such a hard time. But selfishly, the sight of her beautiful face really cheered me up. When the caravan had pulled away from the pastors' house, I thought I would never see any of them again.

I admired Cheri and her willingness to do whatever was necessary to get caught up on her bills. All of the young women in the church were very hard workers; I had seen that time and time again. There was not a lazy one in the bunch. I consider myself to be a hard worker, also, but I felt lazy in comparison to them.

A couple of weeks later, Cheri contacted me and asked if she could stop by my house when I got off work. I was excited to see her once again.

I kept peering out the window, impatient for her to arrive. Her car finally pulled into the driveway. As I watched, she, Nina, Faith and Juanita got out. Juanita had been one of the few that had not made the move to Arizona. I was excited to see her, and very surprised to see the rest of my young friends.

We all hugged and jumped up and down. "I'm so happy to see you all!" I squealed. "I was expecting only Cheri!"

"We wanted to surprise you," Nina said with a smile. "How are you doing?"

It seemed like years since they had left, and at the same time, I felt like I had seen them yesterday. That's how it is with the dearest of friends.

We all filed into my living room and settled in with a cold drink.

Everyone talked at once, laughing and sharing bits of our lives. I was so happy to see my dear friends that I almost cried tears of joy.

"Where's Hannah? Couldn't she come?" I asked.

Hannah had not been able to get away from her part-time job to make the fourteen-hour trek back. "But, I'm going to put her on speaker phone so she can join in our conversation," Cheri said.

Speaker phone? Hmmm.

Cheri cleared her throat. "There's some things we want to talk to you about," she said.

"Okay, I'm ready," I said, steeling myself.

Hannah listened on speaker phone as one by one, the story tumbled out of each of the girls.

The pastors had been leaving for hours at a time to minister in the community, telling one of the young women to look after their children, only to arrive home many hours after they said they would be back. It was always a demand, not a request, and the childcare was expected to be provided for free, of course. The girls were all exhausted and stressed to the breaking point. Somehow they were supposed to pay for groceries and everything else, with no income, and run their lives on faith alone. But that wasn't even the worst part.

Pastor Richard had sexually assaulted two of the young women, and was grooming a third.

I sat in stunned silence. I thought to myself, *no, that's not possible. That could not have happened.*

I trusted these young women with my life. I knew they were not liars. I also knew Pastor Richard was not a liar. So what was the truth?

"We had to move out," Cheri went on. "We found an apartment, and that's where Hannah is staying. But the rest of us are living with my mom, here."

I forced myself to ask the question: "Hannah, are you going to stay there? Are you coming back also?"

On speaker phone, Hannah said the lease on the apartment ended in about six months, and then she was moving out, but at this point, she didn't know where.

I studied each girl's face, and landed on Juanita. "Did you know about this?" I asked her.

She nodded. "That's why I didn't – " and broke off in mid-sentence.

So Juanita had been a victim, too. And it had started before anyone ever left for Arizona.

In a way, it wasn't surprising. These young women were beautiful, talented, successful, and fully invested in the ministry of Boundless Horizons. All of us had been taught, from day one, about the importance of submitting to the ministry and obeying commands.

For me, it had been easy. I loved my pastors with all my heart, and I had seen firsthand the sacrifices they had made for the gospel. It was easy to submit to them.

But I had not been sexually assaulted. I tried to imagine what would have happened if I had. Knowing my fiery temper and my tendency to be quick to anger (both traits warned against in the Bible), I'm afraid that Pastor Richard would have ended up with some teeth missing, and I would have ended up in jail.

The girls went on to talk about the endless financial challenges, the requests from the pastors for them to provide food for the household, when no one was working and no one had any way to buy groceries for nine people, the requests to pay their utility bills, and on and on. I learned that Pastor Leah had secretly asked each person to give a specific amount of money, making it seem as though that was the exact amount she needed to pay a bill, but not telling any of the others that that same amount had been requested from everyone else. When they compared notes, they learned that she had told them all the same story: this is how much I need, and you are the only one who can help me.

All of it had been a lie.

As tempting as it was to blame Pastor Leah for this, I couldn't. I put the blame squarely on Pastor Richard's shoulders. His wife had to sneak around and resort to devious tactics to put food in her children's mouths, because he was not supporting his family.

Like a swirling kaleidoscope, everything seemed to settle into place in my mind. Pastor Leah had lied continually about money, in the eleven years I had known her. How many times had we all heard the words, "I'll pay you back?"

It's very interesting to me that God has created the human psyche to experience opposite, contradicting emotions, at the same time. I loved Pastor Richard, and I loved his commitment to preaching the word. I hated him for assaulting my friends. I loved Pastor Leah for her endless kindness to me, and the endless years she had prayed and fasted for me. I hated her for lying to all of us.

My young friends and I all talked and prayed together. I asked the Lord to heal these young women, and to guide them in the direction they needed to go. Although no one said it out loud, it seemed painfully obvious that, in a moment's time, Boundless Horizons Church had died to all of us.

Over the next few weeks, I packed up all the things that were church property that I had been storing in my house, and sent them FedEx to the pastors' house. I wrote a letter resigning as treasurer and mailed it to them. Every time I came across something I had overlooked previously, I packed it up and sent it off. I wanted nothing in my home connected to those people. With the same zeal that I had served them for eleven years, I now purged myself of every trace of them and their church.

Yet, the love I had in my heart continued to linger for them. I did love them. I couldn't stop loving them. I just could not be a part of their ministry any longer, in any way.

Someone may be thinking, "You didn't leave the ministry; the ministry left you." And in many ways, that's true, of course. But my pastors expected me to continue on as church treasurer, even after they moved out of state. They expected me to continue to do the taxes and the payroll (if any), and all the other necessary bookkeeping tasks. I'm sure they were shocked when they received my resignation letter, but I was truly in fight-or-flight mode. I simply had to flee, flee everything, and flee quickly.

***

Obviously, I had known that all the roles I had played at Boundless Horizons had taken their toll on me. But I didn't realize just how much of a toll it had been.

As the weeks went by, a thought would come to me: Oh, I need to do such-and-such for the church. It would be followed by a profound sense of relief. No, I don't.

The stress and the burdens gradually released from me. I felt as though a thousand-pound rock had rolled off of my shoulders.

Afterword ~ Julia Anshasi

I keep in touch with Amy. Every once in a while I will text her and ask her how she's doing.

Amy is attending a different church in her home city. She likes the pastors and the people, and enjoys the preaching. The pastors seem to genuinely love and serve God.

But Amy has been scarred by her experience in a cult. She wants to get involved at her new church, but remembers how the work was piled on her before, and she's leery about that happening again. She wants to use her God-given talents to help others, but is afraid of being lied to and taken advantage of, once again.

"Amy, what are you going to do?" I asked her one day.

"I don't know," she said slowly. "It seems so strange to me to go from one hundred miles per hour in one ministry, to zero in the next. I know I should be doing something, but I also feel like I need time to heal."

I urged Amy to take time for herself – to immerse herself in God's word daily, to give herself to prayer. I asked her about her former pastors.

"I don't really know what's going on with them," she said nervously. She looked over her shoulder, as though someone might be eavesdropping on our conversation. "I hope they're okay."

Amy shared with me that she had prayed and fasted, and asked God to take away the hatred she had felt toward her former pastors. "And He did," she smiled. "I love them, and I wish only good things for them. But I'm so thankful that He rescued me from that cult."

This was only the second time I had heard Amy use the word cult. I felt it was another step forward for her.

While doing research for this book, I came across a lot of information about cults. I felt a shiver up my back as I read the characteristics of a cult, and how Boundless Horizons Church matched the description precisely. Amy and I went through the information together and had a point-by-point discussion about it, and it was eye-opening.

Characteristics of a Cult (source: easysociology.com)

Cults are defined by several key characteristics:

1. Charismatic Leadership: Cults often revolve around a charismatic leader who is viewed as uniquely insightful, spiritually advanced, or divinely inspired. This leader wields significant influence over the group's beliefs and practices. The leader's charisma often acts as the glue that binds members together, fostering a sense of loyalty and purpose.

2. New or Unconventional Beliefs: Cults typically promote beliefs and practices that deviate from mainstream religious or societal norms. These beliefs are often seen as innovative or revelatory. In many cases, these ideas emerge as a reaction to perceived gaps or limitations in traditional belief systems.

3. High Levels of Commitment: Members of cults are often expected to demonstrate a high degree of commitment, which may include financial contributions, time investment, or even severing ties with non-members. This commitment is often fostered through rigorous rituals, indoctrination practices, and personal sacrifices.

4. Isolation from Broader Society: Many cults create a strong sense of "us versus them," which can lead to social isolation. This helps reinforce group cohesion and loyalty. Isolation also serves as a mechanism for leaders to maintain control over members by limiting external influences.

5. Strong Internal Social Control: Rules and norms within cults are typically rigidly enforced, with nonconformity discouraged or penalized. This ensures the group's survival and the leader's authority. Such control can manifest through surveillance, public shaming, or other forms of coercion.

***

"So, regarding number one, charismatic leadership, do you feel like Pastors Richard and Leah are charismatic?" I asked Amy over a cup of tea one day.

"Oh, yes," she nodded her head vigorously. "When I first started attending, I was really drawn to them because they seemed so different. They showered me with love and attention. Pastor Richard is such a dynamic speaker! He is definitely a hellfire and brimstone kind of preacher. And Pastor Leah is so gentle and loving. I was drawn to her even more. I wanted to be like her."

"What about new or unconventional beliefs?" I asked.

"Pastor Richard always said we could make money through ideas, not by working at a job," Amy explained. "He would often reprimand us for not coming up with new ideas. He would remind us about how social media got started – someone had an idea! And then it just took off, and people made millions from it. My problem was, I just could never come up with any ideas. I also think that's part of the reason why they asked us to leave work in the middle of the day to attend to something the church needed done. It always made me so nervous when they did that! I always felt like they didn't understand what it means to have a job, where you have to report every day, where other people are depending on you.

"Pastor Richard also believed you could supernaturally get a photograph of someone on your phone, if you needed to track that person down, even if you had never had that person's photo on your phone. I would love to see it happen, but I never experienced that.

"One time after service, we were praying, and Pastor Leah told us to look at the palms of our hands. She said one palm would be darker than the other palm. I looked at my hands, and sure enough, one was darker than the other. This freaked me out. What was that all about? What was the purpose of that? Does God do things like that just to show us His power? I don't know."

"I think I know what you're going to say about high levels of commitment," I smiled.

Amy also smiled, ruefully. "High levels doesn't even begin to describe it," she shook her head. "We were all on call 24/7. Church always came first. The pastors and their children were always our top priority. So many of us were in school at that time, and we had to study for tests, or whatever, but we were always being pulled away to do church business. The young women would sometimes go days without sleeping. I refused to do that! And the money! Wow – we gave so many thousands of dollars to that church. We sacrificed our own needs.

"It still really hurts me that the girls gave them all the money they had saved to put a down payment on an apartment. Everyone was just giving, giving, giving, all the time. Money, time, hours spent awake when we should have been sleeping – it was just non-stop giving, to the point that it required a super-human effort to just get through each day."

"What about isolation from broader society?" I asked her.

Amy laughed. "Honestly, with the amount of work that we all did for the church, plus our paying jobs, plus going to school, there was no time to even be involved in broader society. There was just no time.

"They did constantly warn us about associating with people who weren't part of the church. They warned us that those people would bring us down and turn us away from God."

"The last one is strong internal social control," I said. "How do you feel about that aspect?"

"Remember the sparkly dresses I told you about?" Amy laughed. "That was kind of an unwritten rule. Since then, I've looked around at other churches, and I've never seen any that have that type of dress code.

"We did this thing that really bothered me," she went on. "I grew up with some Catholic friends, and when you go to the Catholic Church, the priest says something, and all the people chant back at him. It's always the same words on both sides. I never understood that. But at Boundless Horizons, Pastor Richard would say, 'God is good,' and we all had to say back to him, 'All the time.' Then he would say, 'And all the time,' and we were supposed to say, 'God is good.' It never varied. It was such a mindless chant. Most of the time I didn't participate in it. It didn't make sense to me. But everyone was expected to do it. And not just once per service – sometimes ten times per service!"

Amy, who had been relaxed up to this point, suddenly stiffened and looked over her shoulder. I asked her about it.

"We were always told that if we criticized the ministry, bad things would happen to us." Her voice was barely above a whisper. "The pastors told us that people who criticized them would get sick, end up in the hospital, have a car accident, get arrested, even die. I've always been afraid to say anything to anyone, even the other people in the church. I just didn't know what might happen.

"But things are different now," Amy continued. "Now that I know about what happened with the money, and the assaults, I feel so differently about everything. I feel like it's my obligation to speak out."

At one point, Amy looked so sad, I thought she might cry. I asked her what she was feeling.

"I'm thinking about the girls who worked for Pastor Leah for free," she said, looking at the floor. "They spent months and months, working hours and hours, and never got paid. I don't even know how that's possible.

"Pastor Leah is the perfect Biblical example of a submissive wife," Amy continued. "She will never say one word against her husband – not one word! She had to have known what he was doing with the young women. How could she not know? Maybe she felt that she was in so deep already, with all the unpaid wages and unpaid bills, that a little philandering by her husband was a non-issue. I don't know how she could stand it – I certainly couldn't.

"I still think a lot about Guadalupe, and how much I miss her. Maybe she left because she knew all the stuff that was going on behind the scenes, and she just didn't want to talk about it. She didn't want the drama, or, she didn't want anything terrible to happen to her if she spoke up, as we had all been warned.

"One thing I've been questioning a lot lately is this. What about all the bad things that have happened to Pastors Richard and Leah? They lost a child, Pastor Leah has been hospitalized several times, they have had people threaten to kill them, and they've had people doing witchcraft against them and their children. They've defaulted on so many of their bills and payments; their credit rating is non-existent. I question what their explanation for all this is? If those things happened to someone in the congregation, they would say it was because that person criticized the ministry. But which ministry are they criticizing?"

Amy shook her head. "I believe that bad things happened to all of us. It's true, a lot of the time we bring bad things on ourselves. But sometimes, God has to discipline us. I believe God is disciplining them. It hurts me so much to say that, because I love them so much! But I really believe that's what's happening.

"I wish them all the best. I pray that God will protect them and their children. Most of all, I pray that Pastor Richard will repent for what he did to the girls. That's the most important thing, in my opinion."

I asked Amy if she had any regrets in being a part of Boundless Horizons. Did she wish she had never walked through the door?

"No," Amy said slowly. "I learned so much about the Bible – things I never knew before. I learned the importance of faith, and not giving up. It was all so different from what I was used to! These were things that I really needed to learn.

"I saw people being delivered from demonic influences. I saw people being instantly healed from all kinds of physical problems. I, myself, was miraculously healed several times.

"For me, the main take away is just this: Love your leaders, love the congregation, but don't be afraid to ask questions! If someone is telling you not to ask questions, or telling you that something bad will happen to you if you do, that should be a big red flag to you.

"Even the disciples asked Jesus questions. If the question was wrong, He would rebuke them! It's okay to be rebuked, but threats are another thing.

"I don't regret my time at Boundless Horizons. It made me who I am today. It made me grow up. Some of the happiest memories of my life occurred in that church, with those people."

I am amazed at Amy's courage, and the courage of her friends, to leave the church and make a new life for themselves.

God truly is good, all the time.

If you are trapped in a cult, please seek help. There are many online resources to help you escape. One excellent resource I found is peopleleavecults.com.

There is hope!

Now the Lord is that Spirit: and where the Spirit of the Lord is, there is liberty. 2 Corinthians 3: 17

***

I trust that this book has blessed you. It has blessed me as well! Please visit our website for more resources:

www.giantpublishingcompany.com

www.ingramcontent.com/pod-product-compliance
Lightning Source LLC
Chambersburg PA
CBHW060349190426
43201CB00043B/1893